Congressional
Research
Service

The Lacey Act: Protecting the Environment by Restricting Trade

Kristina Alexander
Legislative Attorney

April 12, 2012

Congressional Research Service

7-5700

www.crs.gov

R42067

CRS Report for Congress
Prepared for Members and Committees of Congress

Summary

The Lacey Act was enacted in 1900 to prevent hunters from killing game in one state and escaping prosecution by crossing state lines. It has evolved into a law that prohibits import, export, transport, purchase, or sale of species when that action would violate state, federal, tribal, or foreign law. Congress amended the Lacey Act most recently in 2008, expanding the reach of the act to include timber and timber products. Implementation of the 2008 Amendments has proved controversial, and the Department of Agriculture Animal and Plant Health Inspection Service (APHIS) initially delayed implementing the act's new declaration requirements for importing wood products.

Some find the Lacey Act puzzling. While people charged with violating the act are charged with violating a U.S. law, that prosecution is premised on a violation of another law, sometimes the law of another country. That has led some to claim that the United States is enforcing the laws of another country. U.S. conservation laws (such as the Lacey Act), however, have long protected species and habitats even outside of the United States. Worldwide conservation was one reason for expanding Lacey Act coverage to more plants in 2008. Preserving U.S. timber jobs and prices was another reason. However, the 2008 Amendments allow enforcement of foreign laws that are not directly related to conservation or U.S. jobs, such as failure to pay foreign stumpage fees, or shipping wood in violation of a country's export restrictions. After search warrants were executed by the Department of the Interior Fish and Wildlife Service (FWS) against Gibson Guitar Corp. of Nashville, TN, apparently based on the possible illegal import of wood from India, Congress has taken another look at whether the 2008 Amendments achieve the goals of the Lacey Act. As introduced in October 2011, H.R. 3210 would amend the act to limit its application to wood imported prior to 2008 and composite wood products, and would allow an innocent owner defense to forfeiture actions. A different approach is taken by H.R. 4171/S. 2062, which would eliminate any reference to violations of foreign laws and end criminal prosecutions for violating the act.

Contents

Figures

Tables

Appendixes

Contacts

Background

The Lacey Act addresses conservation by targeting trade. As adopted in 1900, the Lacey Act made it a federal crime to ship game killed in violation of one state's laws to another state.[1] It also regulated the introduction of non-native species and prohibited shipment of wildlife without clear identification of the contents and shipper.[2] This report will examine the portions of the Lacey Act that pertain to transporting fish, wildlife, and plants that were taken in violation of another law, and will not address the other provisions of the act.

While it has been amended many times since 1900, the Lacey Act's format has remained the same: with respect to fish, wildlife, and plants, generally speaking, it is a violation of the act to violate another law, be it state, federal, tribal, or foreign. Accordingly, making a case under the Lacey Act requires a violation of an underlying law as well as a violation of the act itself.

The act has a broad reach. It applies to any person, with *person* defined to include individuals, corporations, government officials, and government agencies.[3] It covers violations of state, federal, tribal, or foreign laws (including regulations) that regulate "the taking, possession, importation, exportation, transportation, or sale" of wildlife or plants.[4] It is enforced by the Fish and Wildlife Service (FWS) of the Department of the Interior, the National Oceanic and Atmospheric Administration of the Department of Commerce, Customs and Border Protection (CBP) of the Department of Homeland Security, and the Animal and Plant Health Inspection Service (APHIS) and the Forest Service of the Department of Agriculture.[5]

The 2008 Amendments

In 2008, the Lacey Act was amended, expanding the definition of plants to include trees and plant products, and prohibiting different types of trade related to plants. In August 2011, FWS executed search warrants for the premises of Gibson Guitar Corp. reportedly based on Gibson's violations of the 2008 Amendments when Gibson allegedly imported unfinished wood in violation of India's export laws. Because Gibson has claimed its imported wood was sustainably harvested, some argue that the 2008 Amendments do not conserve environmental resources exclusively but can hurt U.S. workers by enforcing foreign laws that protect foreign workers. Others argue that the act protects U.S. jobs. For more discussion on the policy behind the amendments, see CRS Report R42119, *The Lacey Act: Compliance Issues Related to Importing Plants and Plant Products*, by Pervaze A. Sheikh.

---

[1] Act of May 25, 1900, §3, 31 Stat. 187.

[2] Act of May 25, 1900, §2 and §4, respectively, 31 Stat. 188.

[3] 16 U.S.C. §3371(e).

[4] 16 U.S.C. §3371(d).

[5] See 16 U.S.C. §3371(h) (defining Secretary as the Secretary of the Interior and the Secretary of Agriculture); 16 U.S.C. §3373(a) (stating that the provisions will be enforced by "the Secretary, the Secretary of Transportation, or the Secretary of the Treasury").

Legislative History of the 2008 Amendments

According to the legislative history for the 2008 amendments, its purposes were two-fold: to promote ecosystem protection and to aid the U.S. timber industry. According to the House Conference Report, the amendments address the following problems:

> [I]llegal logging undermines responsible forest enterprises by distorting timber markets with unfair competition and price undercutting. Illegal logging also threatens the conservation of forest resources, wildlife, and biodiversity, by facilitating forest conversion to non-forest uses and depleting or completely eliminating certain forest ecosystems or the habitat of certain forest dependent wildlife. Finally, illegal logging results in a loss of revenue when taxes or royalties are not paid that could otherwise be invested in sustainable forest management or economic development.[6]

Senator Wyden, a co-sponsor of a bill that led to the 2008 Amendments described the benefits of the act as follows: "This legislation will raise the risks for illegal trade without harming legal trade and will be an important step toward leveling a playing field currently stacked against the U.S. forest products industry and importers and retailers committed to trading in legal wood products."[7]

Senator Alexander, another co-sponsor, discussed the bill's projected economic impact of illegal timber imports: "[I]t is an estimated $1 billion a year in depressed prices and reduced exports. It depresses prices $500 million to $700 million annually. It means the people who play by the rules in the United States are having money taken from them by criminals who don't play by the rules in other countries ..."[8]

Prohibitions Related to Wildlife

Because of the complexity of the act, involving federal, state, and/or foreign laws, the act is best analyzed with respect to the type of goods it seeks to protect. This report will first look at those parts of the Lacey Act pertaining to wildlife. Plants will be discussed later in the context of the 2008 Amendments. However, as will be discussed in greater detail below, with respect to both wildlife and plants, penalties for Lacey Act violations are based on the degree of knowledge or care taken by the alleged offender, while forfeiture of protected wildlife and plants under the Lacey Act is on a strict liability basis.

Violations of U.S. or Tribal Law

The act uses the term *fish or wildlife* to include "any wild animal, whether living or dead ... [including] any part, product, egg, or offspring thereof."[9] This report will simply use the term *wildlife*. There are two types of prohibited acts pertaining to wildlife. The first makes it illegal to "import, export, transport, sell, receive, acquire, or purchase" wildlife if that creature was "taken, possessed, transported, or sold in violation of any law ... of the United States or in violation of

---

[6] H.Rept. 110-627; 1981 USCCAN p. 127, 536. (May 13, 2008).

[7] S. Cong. Rec. 15622, at 15635 (December 14, 2007).

[8] S. Cong. Rec. at 13968 (November 6, 2007).

[9] 16 U.S.C. §3371(a).

any Indian tribal law."[10] In this case, a violation of a federal law that regulates wildlife is also a violation of the Lacey Act if the wildlife in question was imported, exported, transported, sold, or received.

Example[11] 1 (Section 3372(a)(1))

Assume a person has killed a hummingbird in the state of Oklahoma. That is a violation of the Migratory Bird Treaty Act (MBTA), a federal law.[12] However, it is not a violation of the Lacey Act. Even though wild ife was taken in violation of a federal law, that wildlife was not then imported, exported, transported, sold, received, acquired, or purchased, as required for a Lacey Act violation.

Example 2 (Section 3372(a)(1))

Assume a person has killed a hummingbird in the state of Oklahoma. That person has violated the MBTA. That person then sells the feathers to a person in Oklahoma. By making the sale, that person has also violated the Lacey Act because there was a sale of wild ife (which by definition includes parts of that animal) that was taken in violation of a federal law. The buyer also has violated the Lacey Act because the buyer purchased wildlife that was taken in violation of a federal law.

Violations of State or Foreign Law

The second type of wildlife prohibition under the Lacey Act involves interstate or foreign commerce. Section 3372(a)(2)(A) of the Lacey Act makes it illegal to "import, export, transport, sell, receive, acquire, or purchase in interstate or foreign commerce" wildlife if that wildlife was "taken, possessed, transported, or sold in violation of any law or regulation of any State or in violation of any foreign law."[13] For this type of violation, the underlying law must be state or foreign. While the language clearly includes state regulatory violations as a predicate act to a Lacey Act violation ("in violation of any law or regulation of any State"), it is not so clear from the statute whether violations of foreign regulations may also be the basis for a Lacey Act violation. Courts, however, have held that foreign regulations may be the foundation for a charge. The Eleventh Circuit reviewed congressional intent before holding that violations of foreign regulations and other legally binding provisions are also a basis for making a Lacey Act enforcement case.[14] The Ninth Circuit found that Congress used the term "foreign law" so it would encompass the many forms that foreign legal edicts may take.[15]

---

[10] 16 U.S.C. §3372(a)(1).

[11] The *Examples* in this report should be considered hypothetical situations and not factually or legally true.

[12] 16 U.S.C. §703(a).

[13] 16 U.S.C. §3372(a)(2)(A).

[14] See United States v. McNab, 331 F.3d 1228 (11th Cir. 2003).

[15] United States v. 594,464 Pounds of Salmon, 871 F.2d 824, 826 (9th Cir. 1989).

Example 3 (Section 3372(a)(2)(A))

Assume a person has killed a deer in violation of Wisconsin's hunting laws. The deer is field dressed and consumed without leaving the state or entering commerce. There is no violation of the Lacey Act because there is no interstate commerce.

Example 4 (Section 3372(a)(2)(A))

Assume a person has killed a deer in violation of Wisconsin's hunting laws by hunting in an area where it is not allowed, for example, a petting zoo. The venison is sold to a person in interstate commerce. Because interstate commerce was involved, the seller has violated the Lacey Act. Likewise, the buyer also has violated the Lacey Act.

The Lacey Act has an expanded use of the term *sale* in the context of wildlife violations. It deems an offer to provide guiding or outfitting services, or to provide a hunting or fishing license or permit as a sale.[16] Accordingly, obtaining a hunting license in violation of tribal law can be the predicate violation of the Lacey Act.[17]

Before a violation occurs under either Section 3372(a)(1) or Section 3372(a)(2)(A), both parts of the Lacey Act must be triggered—the underlying or predicate law and then the Lacey Act. Courts must determine the validity of both the predicate violation and the action that triggers the Lacey Act charge. Where the predicate violation is one of foreign law or regulation, the federal courts have the authority to determine whether a foreign law has been violated.[18] Federal courts also have jurisdiction when the underlying violation is one of tribal law.[19]

Establishing violations of foreign law can lead to complicated situations. For example, the United States seized the hide and horns of an Afghan Urial, a type of big horn sheep, imported to Virginia from Pakistan. The importer of the animal argued that Pakistan had no national law protecting the Urial and that he had a valid permit from the province where it was taken. The Fifth Circuit held that a Pakistani law that prohibited the export of wild animal hides barred the export of the Urial pelt.[20] In another case a man was convicted of importing spiny lobsters to the United States that were caught in violation of Honduras law. By the time the conviction was appealed, "the Honduran government reversed its position; it [refuted] the validity of the laws it previously verified."[21] The Eleventh Circuit held that Honduras law at the time the conduct occurred prohibited harvesting the spiny lobsters and upheld the Lacey Act conviction.[22]

---

[16] 16 U.S.C. §3372(c).

[17] See United States v. March, 111 Fed. Appx. 888 (9th Cir. 2004).

[18] Fed. R. Civ. P. 44.1: "… In determining foreign law, the court may consider any relevant material or source, including testimony, whether or not submitted by a party or admissible under the Federal Rules of Evidence. The court's determination must be treated as a ruling on a question of law."

[19] United States v. March, 111 Fed. Appx. 888 (9th Cir. 2004).

[20] United States v. One Afghan Urial Ovis Orientalis Blanfordi Fully Mounted Sheep, 964 F.2d 474 (5th Cir. 1992).

[21] United States v. McNab, 331 F 3d 1228, 1232 (11th Cir. 2003).

[22] United States v. McNab, 331 F 3d 1228, 1242 (11th Cir. 2003).

In determining that the predicate violation occurred, the court does not have to find that the procedures of that jurisdiction were followed. Federal procedural rules apply.[23] For example, the Fourth Circuit has held that the general federal statute of limitations applies.[24] For a Lacey Act violation, there is a five-year statute of limitations.[25]

Prohibitions Related to Plants

The Lacey Act definition of plant was expanded in 2008 to include any wild member of the plant kingdom including roots, seeds, parts, or products, including trees.[26] Prior to the 2008 Amendments, the Lacey Act applied only to those plants that were indigenous to the United States and listed under one of the following: the Endangered Species Act (ESA); the Convention on International Trade in Endangered Species of Wild Fauna and Flora (CITES); or a state law to conserve species threatened with extinction.[27] It did not expressly apply to plant products. The revised definition has some exclusions, such as for scientific research and for plants that will be transplanted.[28] The Lacey Act prohibits four types of acts related to plants and requires submission of a declaration for importing plants.

Violations of U.S. or Tribal Law

One prohibited activity is identical for plant violations as it is for wildlife violations. The Lacey Act makes it illegal to "import, export, transport, sell, receive, acquire, or purchase" plants if the plant was "taken, possessed, transported, or sold in violation of [U.S. or Indian tribal law]."[29] As for the wildlife violations, these cases tend to be fact-specific. For example, the saguaro cactus, an icon of the American Southwest, is not protected under federal law but is under Arizona State law. Accordingly, taking a saguaro cactus would not be a Lacey Act violation under Section 3372(a)(1),[30] but would be under Section 3372(a)(2)(B), as discussed below.

---

[23] See United States v. Thomas, 887 F.2d 1341, 1348-49 (9th Cir. 1989) (holding that the federal five-year statute of limitations applied, not the state one-year statute of limitations).

[24] United States v. Borden, 10 F.3d 1058, 1062 (4th Cir. 1993) (rejecting the argument that the state one-year statute of limitations applied).

[25] 18 U.S.C. §3282(a). See Agency Holding Corp. v. Malley-Duff & Assocs., Inc., 483 U.S. 143, 155 (1987) (holding in a RICO case that "if no statute specifically defines a limitations period ... for a particular offense, a 'catchall' statute operates to forbid prosecution, trial, or punishment 'unless the indictment is found or the information is instituted within five years next after such offense shall have been committed'").

[26] 16 U.S.C. §3371(f).

[27] Prior to enactment of the 2008 Amendments, the act defined *plant* as: "any wild member of the plant kingdom, including roots, seeds, and other parts thereof (but excluding common food crops and cultivars) which is indigenous to any State and which is either (A) listed on an appendix to the Convention on International Trade in Endangered Species of Wild Fauna and Flora, or (B) listed pursuant to any State law that provides for the conservation of species threatened with extinction." 16 U.S.C. §3371(f) (2007).

[28] The regulatory definitions of common food crops and cultivars have not completed the rulemaking process. A draft definition was issued on August 4, 2010. 75 Fed. Reg. 46859.

[29] 16 U.S.C. §3372(a)(1).

[30] See United States v. Miller, 981 F.2d 439 (9th Cir. 1992) (case pre-dating the 2008 Amendments).

Example 5 (Section 3372(a)(1))

A person in New York found sandplain gerardia on federal lands, a plant listed as endangered under the ESA. That person kills the plant. The person has violated the ESA,[31] but has not violated the Lacey Act because there has been no act of import, export, transport, sale, receipt, acquisition, or purchase of the plant.

Example 6 (Section 3372(a)(1))

A person digs up a Kuenzler hedgehog cactus (an endangered species) from a state park, which violates state law, and sells it to someone in another state. The buyer plants it in the perfect spot and it flourishes. Even though the plant does not die, there is still a violation of the ESA, which prohibits digging up endangered plants in violation of state law, as well as buying or selling them in interstate commerce.[32] Therefore, both the seller and the buyer have violated the ESA. Because there was a sale, both have also violated the Lacey Act.

Violations of State or Foreign Law Protecting Plants

The 2008 Amendments added three other prohibited acts related to plants. The first directly relates to laws that conserve plants. It prohibits importing, exporting, transporting, selling, receiving, acquiring, or purchasing any plant in interstate or foreign commerce if that plant was taken, possessed, transported, or sold in violation of state or foreign laws that

1. protect plants;

2. regulate the theft of plants;

3. regulate the taking of plants from a park, forest reserve, or other officially protected area;

4. regulate the taking of plants from an officially designated area; or

5. regulate the taking of plants without, or contrary to, required authorization.[33]

Under this section, Section 3372(a)(2)(B)(i), it is illegal to take a plant, including a tree or a plant product, in interstate commerce, if the state or foreign country protected the specific plant in some way or protected the area from which the plant was taken, and that protection was violated. Under the 2008 Amendments, taking a saguaro cactus, as discussed above, would be prosecuted under Section 3372(a)(2)(B).

---

[31] 16 U.S.C. §1538(a)(2).

[32] 16 U.S.C. §1538(a)(2).

[33] 16 U.S.C. §3372(a)(2)(B).

Example 7 (Section 3372(a)(2)(B)(i))

A person takes wild sage leaves from the roadside of Turkey, and then brings the leaves into the United States for the person's own use. Assume it is against Turkish law to pick sage leaves off roadside plants without authorization. A Lacey Act violation occurred because the person imported sage leaves that violated a foreign law.

Example 8 (Section 3372(a)(2)(B)(i))

A person picks leaves of a plant that grows only in Turkey from the roadside and then brings the leaves into the United States to sell. Assume this violates Turkish law. Assume it is against U.S. law to sell those leaves. Prior to enactment of the 2008 Amendments there would be no Lacey Act violation, as the definition of *plant* at the time required that the plant be indigenous to the United States (or listed under ESA, CITES, or state law) for the prohibitions to apply, and underlying foreign law was not applicable in the pre-2008 Lacey Act.

Violations of State or Foreign Law Requiring Fees

The other two plant prohibitions are less directly linked to conservation. One prohibition under the 2008 Amendments makes it illegal to import, export, transport, sell, receive, acquire, or purchase a plant in interstate or foreign commerce that was "taken, possessed, transported, or sold without the payment of appropriate royalties, taxes, or stumpage fees required for the plant by any law or regulation of any State or any foreign law."[34] Under this provision, the type of plant or the location of the plant is not at issue. The predicate act is based on whether the plant was harvested legally in relation to required fees. Prohibiting import, export, sales, and purchases of timber based on payment of fees could be argued as having a conservation interest by limiting illegally harvested trees, even if the illegality is related to paying fees, rather than the type or locale of the trees. The theory that this prohibition supports conservation is that lawless harvesting limits the economic advantage timber harvesting typically brings, such as funds for reforestation or other protections.[35] From an enforcement perspective, these violations can be easier to prove because there will be paperwork showing whether the fees were paid (as opposed to proof of illegal origin, for example), and the conservation benefits can more easily be realized.

Example 9 (Section 3372(a)(2)(B)(ii))

An American furniture manufacturer imports oak from Canada knowing that the price is good because the timber company selling the wood "knows a guy" who can avoid paying fees for cutting the trees. The American furniture company has violated the Lacey Act even though it was the timber company or "the guy" that did not pay the fees. The act prohibits purchase of timber taken or sold without paying appropriate taxes and royalties. It does not have to be the purchaser or importer that was required to pay the fees.

---

[34] 16 U.S.C. §3372(a)(2)(B)(ii).

[35] See Cong. Rec. E533 (March 13, 2007) (Rep. Blumenauer: "By avoiding export duties, timber royalties and taxes on their profits, companies operating unlawfully are robbing national governments of in excess of $15 billion annually on public lands alone. This loss in revenue decreases governments' ability to invest in the forestry sector to promote sustainable forest management and conserve their natural forest resources").

Violations of State or Foreign Law Restricting Export

The last prohibition added by the 2008 Amendments makes it illegal to import, export, transport, sell, receive, acquire, or purchase a plant in interstate or foreign commerce that was "taken, possessed, transported, or sold in violation of any limitation under any law or regulation of any State, or under any foreign law, governing the export or transshipment of plants."[36] Because there is no specific requirement that the export law relate to conservation, some could contend this provision is more likely to preserve trade advantages, rather than to protect ecosystems. But the argument could be made that any restriction of trade in wood and wood products provides conservation benefit by potentially limiting the amount of wood that is harvested and exported. These export laws can serve as an enforcement "choke point" for that jurisdiction. Local officials can moderate how the wood being processed was taken, thus serving a conservation purpose. For example, by reviewing wood finishing, the foreign government has the opportunity to review harvesting issues, such as location and types of wood. Another conservation benefit to enforcing foreign export laws can be illustrated by the example of a country with a limited supply of a type of wood but an unlimited demand for that wood worldwide. If processing were allowed to occur outside of the country, that rare timber would be harvested without any limitation. By requiring local processing, harvest is limited to the speed of domestic manufacturing, thus conserving the timber. These provisions may also aid U.S. timber industry interests by restricting imported wood and wood products.

Example 10 (Section 3372(a)(2)(B)(iii))

Under the law of a foreign country, only hand-made toothpicks may be exported. That same country has no restrictions on harvesting a common tree. A U.S. importer imports machine-made toothpicks, made of that common tree. The importer has violated the Lacey Act because it has imported plants (or plant products) in violation of a foreign law governing export of plants.

Declaration

The 2008 Amendments also added a requirement for a declaration to be prepared by those importing plants under the act. Under Section 3372(f), after a period of time following enactment of the amendments (which occurred May 22, 2008), it became illegal to import a plant (or plant product) without a declaration showing the following:

- the scientific name (including genus and species);
- the value;
- the quantity, including unit of measure; and
- the country from which the plant was taken.[37]

The declaration is submitted by the importer at the time of import. A copy of the form is maintained in either electronic or paper form by APHIS and CBP.

---

[36] 16 U.S.C. §3372(a)(2)(B)(iii).

[37] 16 U.S.C. §3372(f)(1).

The 2008 Amendments required the declaration as of December 15, 2008. However, in response to concerns about the complexity of implementing the declaration requirement, especially for importers of wood products, APHIS established a delayed enforcement schedule, setting compliance stages for some more complicated products for April 1, 2010.[38] Certain products, such as wooden furniture, still are not on an enforcement schedule. (See the **Appendix** for the Schedule.) While the declarations were required for all products as of December 15, 2008, APHIS said it would not prosecute for failure to have a declaration until the dates indicated in the implementation schedule.[39]

The 2008 Amendments also required APHIS to evaluate the declaration process within two years of enactment.[40] In February 2011, APHIS published a notice that it was initiating its review and seeking comments on the implementation of declarations.[41] A report must be submitted to Congress within six months of completing the review.[42]

Penalties: Civil Violations, Felonies, Misdemeanors, and Forfeiture

While Section 3372 states what actions are not legal, Section 3373 tells what actions may be punished. The Lacey Act provides for civil and criminal penalties as well as forfeiture of the protected item. Some conduct can be subject to either civil or criminal charges. The choice is left to the prosecutors at the Department of Justice. These provisions took shape when the Lacey Act was significantly amended in 1981.[43]

Civil Violations

For the violations described in the examples above (as opposed to marking or labeling violations) the standard for a civil violation is whether the person engaged in that conduct "in the exercise of due care should know that the fish or wildlife or plants were taken, possessed, transported, or sold in violation of, or in a manner unlawful under, any underlying law, treaty, or regulation."[44] If so, that person may be assessed "a civil penalty by the Secretary of not more than $10,000 for each such violation."[45] The penalty is reduced if the value of the wildlife or plants is less than $350.[46]

The *exercise of due care* is a common legal phrase meaning the amount of attention a reasonable person in the same circumstances would use. Under this standard, a first-time buyer of imported animals, for example, is likely to be found to have less responsibility than an importer of those

---

[38] 74 Fed. Reg. 45415 (September 2, 2009).

[39] 74 Fed. Reg. at 45416 (September 2, 2009).

[40] 16 U.S.C. §3372(f)(4).

[41] 76 Fed. Reg. 10874 (February 28, 2011).

[42] 16 U.S.C. §3372(f)(5).

[43] P.L. 97-79.

[44] 16 U.S.C. §3373(a)(1). Pursuant to Debt Collection Improvement Act of 1996 (P.L. 104-134) this penalty may be increased by the agency by publishing a notice in the *Federal Register*.

[45] 16 U.S.C. §3373(a)(1).

[46] 16 U.S.C. §3373(a)(1).

animals. It does not excuse deliberate ignorance. Due care requires what is reasonable, such as asking questions. The Senate Report supporting the 1981 Amendments described the standard as follows: "Due care simply requires that a person facing a particular set of circumstances undertake[s] certain steps which a reasonable man would take to do his best to insure that he is not violating the law."[47]

According to that Senate Report, the due care requirement was added to avoid overzealous prosecution of unknowing violators: "The civil penalty provisions are included with the understanding that they will not be administered to penalize innocent purchasers or consumers, but rather with the clear intent that they will be applied fairly in an equitable and nonabusive manner."[48]

Misdemeanors

Similarly, the Lacey Act makes it a criminal misdemeanor for someone "who knowingly engages in conduct prohibited by any provision of this chapter,"[49] and "in the exercise of due care should know that the fish or wildlife or plants were taken, possessed, transported, or sold in violation of, or in a manner unlawful under, any underlying law, treaty or regulation."[50] The criminal misdemeanor provision explicitly requires that the action that triggers the Lacey Act violation be *knowingly* done. This means that the person must know he (or she) is doing the action, such as transporting the item or buying a wildlife or plant product, not that he knows he is doing something wrong.

For the predicate act, the standard for a misdemeanor, like the civil provision, is based on a *due care* standard: it applies to those who "in the exercise of due care should know" that something illegal was occurring. According to that same 1981 Senate Report, this provision was included to avoid leaving "too much potential for abuse and indiscriminate enforcement efforts."[51]

Returning to *Example Two*, above, for illustration, proving the Lacey Act portion of the illegal feather purchase would require the buyer to know only that he was buying a wildlife or plant product, not that he knew he was buying illegal hummingbird feathers. But the predicate violation must also be proved—a court must find that the buyer in the exercise of due care should know that the product was somehow illegal.

---

[47] S. Rept. 97-123; 1981 U.S.C.C.A.N. 1748, 1757-58.

[48] S. Rept. 97-123; 1981 U.S.C.C.A.N. 1748, 1757.

[49] 16 U.S.C. §3373(d)(2)—but not marking or labeling offenses.

[50] 16 U.S.C. §3373(d)(2).

[51] S. Rept. 97-123; 1981 U.S.C.C.A.N. 1748, 1750.

Example 2A—Expanded to Consider Misdemeanor Culpability

A person buys a bag of feathers that includes some hummingbird feathers mixed in with legal goose down. It was the same price as every other bag of down. The person knowingly bought feathers, but in the exercise of due care he would have no knowledge that the feathers he bought were illegal. It is un ikely that a court would find the person by exercising due care should have known he was buying feathers that were taken in violation of federal law.

Example 2B—Expanded to Consider Misdemeanor Culpability

A person buys three tiny green feathers for the same price as a whole bag of down. This person also knowingly committed the act that triggers the Lacey Act by buying the feathers. It is likely that a court would find that this person when buying those tiny feathers did not exercise due care to discover whether a law had been violated. Two factors a court might expect a reasonable person to consider under the circumstances are that the feathers were unusual and that they were more expensive. The failure to ask reasonable questions could support a finding that the second buyer engaged in conduct prohibited by the act (buying feathers) and that any due care would have revealed that the feathers were taken in violation of law, establishing a Lacey Act violation.

A misdemeanor may be punished by up to one year in jail, in addition to or instead of the fine. Despite the Lacey Act authorizing a maximum $10,000 fine for the misdemeanor, under the Criminal Fines Improvement Act, the maximum criminal penalty is adjusted to $100,000 for an individual, and $200,000 for an organization.[52]

Felonies

The felony provision has a higher standard of culpability. Like the misdemeanor provision, it also requires the actor to know he or she was committing the action that triggers the Lacey Act violation—importing, exporting, engaging in the conduct to sell or purchase or attempt to sell or purchase an item taken in violation of another law—but it also requires that the actor know "that the fish or wildlife or plants were taken, possessed, transported, or sold in violation of, or in a manner unlawful under, any underlying law, treaty or regulation."[53] To be a felony there must be knowledge and one of two things: import or export;[54] or commercial conduct and a value of over $350.[55] These requirements were included to avoid imposing big penalties on smaller offenders, according to the 1981 Senate Report.[56] Additionally, that report indicates congressional intent to allow innocent violators to escape criminal prosecution, "the act's criminal culpability requirement assures that innocent violators of the act will not be subject to criminal penalties."[57] Punishment for committing a felony includes incarceration of no more than five years, a fine of $250,000 for individuals and $500,000 for organizations, or both.[58]

---

[52] The Criminal Fines Improvement Act of 1987 enhances criminal fines for those laws whose criminal fines have not been adjusted since 1987. The Criminal Fines Improvement Act applies two steps: first, classification of the offense based on the length of the incarceration provided by the underlying act (18 U.S.C. §3559); and second, calculation of the fine based on the offense classification (18 U.S.C. §3571).

[53] 16 U.S.C. §3373(d)(1).

[54] 16 U.S.C. §3373(d)(1)(A).

[55] 16 U.S.C. §3373(d)(1)(B).

[56] S. Rept. 97-123; 1981 U.S.C.C.A.N. 1748, 1758.

[57] S. Rept. 97-123; 1981 U.S.C.C.A.N. 1748, 1759.

[58] 16 U.S.C. §3373(d)(1). The Lacey Act indicates a maximum fine of $20,000. The fines in the text are based on the (continued...)

To illustrate the felony provisions, consider *Example 4*, above, in which an Illinois buyer purchased a deer killed in violation of Wisconsin law. The court must find the buyer knew two elements: (1) that he was buying something; and (2) that the venison he was buying was illegal in some way.

Example 4A—Expanded to Consider Felony Culpability

The buyer purchased the venison at a farmers' market in November (a time when most, if not all states, allow deer hunting). He paid the going rate for the meat. Under this example, a court likely would find that the buyer had not criminally violated the Lacey Act. Everything was consistent with a bona fide purchase. A reasonable person would not know in these circumstances that the venison was tainted, nor in the exercise of due care would discover the underlying violation of law.

Example 4B—Expanded to Consider Felony Liability

The buyer, an avid deer hunter, purchased the fresh venison at midnight in the parking lot of a petting zoo where remains of the deer could be seen in a pile. The price was very cheap and the seller was wearing a mask. It seems likely a court would find the buyer had criminally violated the Lacey Act. The circumstances of the sale/purchase would cause a reasonable person to know something was wrong.

Forfeiture

The Lacey Act also authorizes forfeiture of the illegal items. Forfeiture is where the government confiscates an item involved in a crime.[59] As the Ninth Circuit found in *United States v. 144,744 Pounds of Blue King Crab,* under the law, the illegally taken or imported item is considered contraband, even if possessing it would not otherwise be illegal.[60] If the forfeiture action is civil, the court does not have to find a person liable for wrongdoing. For example, in the case discussed earlier of the Urial (the big horn sheep from Pakistan), the suit was not against the importer for violating the Lacey Act, but was a case where the government seized the hide and horns from the importer.[61] The prosecution was against the contraband itself. Cases in which civil forfeiture is the only issue have case names where the item is named as the defendant. For criminal forfeiture actions, a successful suit requires conviction of the person who owned the contraband.

Forfeiture can serve two purposes: remedial or punitive. According to the Supreme Court, the remedial purposes include preventing forbidden merchandise from circulating, and reimbursing the government for investigation and enforcement expenses.[62] The punitive goals of forfeiture apply to criminal proceedings.

The Lacey Act applies civil forfeiture proceedings to "all fish or wildlife or plants imported, exported, transported, sold, received, acquired, or purchased contrary to [Section 3372 of the act]

(...continued)

enhanced amounts under the Criminal Fines Improvement Act.

[59] For a broader analysis of forfeiture, see CRS Report 97-139, *Crime and Forfeiture*, by Charles Doyle.

[60] United States v. 144,774 Pounds of Blue King Crab, 410 F.3d 1131 (9th Cir. 2005) (holding that crab taken illegally was property that was illegal to possess and therefore fit the definition of contraband).

[61] United States v. One Afghan Urial Ovis Orientalis Blanfordi Fully Mounted Sheep, 964 F.2d 474 (5th Cir. 1992).

[62] One Lot Emerald Cut Stones v. United States, 409 U.S. 232, 237 (1972).

... notwithstanding any culpability requirements for civil penalty assessment or criminal prosecution [under Section 3373 of the act]."[63] In situations where the wildlife or plants were part of a "criminal violation of this Act for which a felony conviction is obtained," the act allows civil forfeiture of the "vessels, vehicles, aircraft, and other equipment" used in committing the crime.[64]

Prior to the 2008 Amendments, courts held that there was no innocent owner defense to forfeiture under the Lacey Act. These decisions are based on the act's language that that "*all* fish or wildlife or plants [that violate Section 3372] shall be subject to forfeiture ... "[65] According to the 1981 Senate Report, forfeiture was to occur regardless of culpability: "The strict liability forfeiture section of these amendments would allow the protection of various species from harmful illegal trade by withdrawing illegal shipments from the marketplace even when the violation itself is inadvertent."[66]

The only defense described in that report was where the merchandise was without taint and the import ran afoul of the law only in a "minor, technical" manner.[67]

The Fifth Circuit pointed to that legislative background in finding that "the legislative history establishes that the forfeiture statute provides for strict liability, thereby eliminating any 'innocent owner' defense."[68] A federal court in Florida held that the Lacey Act does not provide for an innocent owner defense.[69] As referenced above, in *United States v. 144,744 Pounds of Blue King Crab*, the Ninth Circuit has held that Lacey Act goods are contraband.[70]

The 2008 Amendments added the statement that civil forfeiture was to be "in accordance with the procedure established under [18 U.S.C. §§981-986]."[71] Under this statute, the Civil Asset Forfeiture Reform Act (CAFRA),[72] the government has the burden of proof by a preponderance of evidence.[73] The person owning the forfeited goods may also seek immediate release of the property pending trial.[74]

CAFRA allows a defense to a civil forfeiture for innocent owners, bona fide purchasers, and heirs.[75] However, under CAFRA, the innocent owner defense cannot be used for contraband. The exclusion states: "no person may assert an ownership interest under this subsection in contraband or other property that it is illegal to possess."[76] As discussed above, the Ninth Circuit found that

---

[63] 16 U.S.C. §3374(a)(1).

[64] 16 U.S.C. §3374(a)(2).

[65] 16 U.S.C. §3374(a)(1) (emphasis added).

[66] S. Rept. 97-123; 1981 U.S.C.C.A.N. 1748, 1760.

[67] S. Rept. 97-123; 1981 U.S.C.C.A.N. 1748, 1760.

[68] United States v. One Afghan Urial Ovis Orientalis Blanfordi Fully Mounted Sheep, 964 F.2d 474, 476 (5th Cir. 1992). See also United States v. 2,507 Live Canary Winged Parakeets, 689 F. Supp. 1106, 1117 (S.D. Fla. 1988).

[69] United States v. Proceeds from Sale of Approximately 15,538 Panulirus Argus Lobster Tails, 834 F. Supp. 385 (S.D. Fla. 1993).

[70] United States v. 144,774 Pounds of Blue King Crab, 410 F.3d 1131 (9th Cir. 2005).

[71] 16 U.S.C. §3374(d).

[72] P.L. 106-185.

[73] 18 U.S.C. §983(c)

[74] 18 U.S.C. §983(f).

[75] 18 U.S.C. §983(d).

[76] 18 U.S.C. §983(d)(4).

goods taken in violation of the Lacey Act are contraband. Additionally, the 1981 Senate Report described the goods in the same way: "The act provides for forfeiture of the fish, wildlife and plants on a strict liability basis because the merchandise is, in effect, contraband."[77]

A statement in the House Report on the 2008 Amendments further references the *Blue King Crab* decision to note that incorporating CAFRA by reference may not provide a defense to the strict liability forfeiture provisions under the Lacey Act because of the ruling that goods are contraband under the act.[78]

However, it is possible to have the goods returned while the matter is still administrative, before it is referred to court. This is known as remission. Department of the Interior regulations that apply to forfeitures allow the possibility of remission in administrative forfeitures in rare circumstances. When FWS notifies a person that goods are forfeited, that person may file a petition for remission rather than a claim, which would refer the matter to court. Under 50 C.F.R. §12.24(f), the regulations provide that "If the Solicitor finds the existence of such mitigation circumstances," goods may be remitted. The only published decision available regarding forfeiture of plant products following the 2008 Amendments considered such a petition before rejecting it.[79] According to that administrative case, the Solicitor considered "whether the facts demonstrate a person's honest and good faith intent to comply with the law, their diligence and efforts to comply, and whether the facts tend to show a lack of negligence or moral culpability for whatever failure or mistake is involved in the non-compliance ... "[80] This administrative forfeiture process appears consistent with the legislative discussion of allowing release of untainted goods related to innocent trade violations.

Example 11—Forfeiture of Contraband

While visiting Nicaragua, a couple buys a table made of a rare wood protected under U.S. law. When they enter the United States they lie on the customs declaration, saying the table was a different, non-protected species. They have violated the Lacey Act under Section 3372(a)(1), by transporting an item in violation of U.S. law by lying on a customs declaration. In addition to any civil or criminal prosecution against the couple, the table is contraband and may be seized by the government.

Gibson Guitars and the 2008 Amendments

In August 2011, FWS executed search warrants at Gibson Guitar Corp. premises and seized wood imported from India. Reportedly, the FWS agents were armed. It does not appear any arrests were made at the time. According to a statement from Gibson, the wood was certified by the Forest Stewardship Council[81] as sustainably harvested and was seized by FWS because it was "not

---

[77] S. Rept. 97-123; 1981 U.S.C.C.A.N. 1748, 1760.

[78] H.Rept. 110-882.

[79] U.S. Department of the Interior v. Three Pallets of Tropical Hardwood (Crouch), INV. No. 2009403072, at 3 (Office of the DOI Solicitor June 22, 2010).

[80] U.S. Department of the Interior v. Three Pallets of Tropical Hardwood (Crouch), INV. No. 2009403072, at 4 (Office of the DOI Solicitor June 22, 2010). The Solicitor found no mitigating circumstances "[the importer] did not do all he could within his power to comply with regulations and ensure that the shipment was authorized by an export permit that properly documented the required information." *Id.* at 6.

[81] The Forest Stewardship Council (FSC) is a non-profit group that reviews forest management and production practices. It describes its certification as providing a basis "for socially and environmentally responsible purchasing (continued...)

finished by Indian workers."[82] FWS and the Department of Justice (DOJ) are not commenting on the case.

Section 3375(b) of the Lacey Act authorizes federal agents to carry firearms when enforcing the act. It also allows execution of search and arrest warrants, including searching any vessels, packages, containers, documents, or permits related to the action.

Background

To make sense of the statements in the affidavit prepared to obtain the search warrants, it helps to have some background of relevant trade terminology. Countries generally use the International Harmonized Commodity Description and Coding System (HS) to identify items being shipped. The United States implements the HS in the Harmonized Tariff Schedule of the United States (HTS). Therefore, where the shipment is of foreign origin, it will be identified with HS. Whether HS or HTS, the numbers correlate to the same items. The APHIS chart in the **Appendix** uses HTS numbers to identify what wood products required a declaration by what date.

For the purposes of the Gibson investigation, two HS codes are relevant. The first is HS 4407—wood split lengthwise that is greater than 6 mm thick. The second is HS 4408—wood veneers, less than 6 mm thick. According to a U.S. customs ruling in 1993, fingerboards for musical instruments, such as guitars and violins, are covered under HS 4407, meaning they are greater than 6 mm thick.[83] Veneer is defined by *Webster's New Collegiate Dictionary* as "a thin sheet of a material: a layer of wood of superior value or excellent grain to be glued to an inferior wood."

According to the affidavit prepared to obtain the Gibson search warrants, "India prohibits the export of products classified under HS Code 4407 for all plant species harvested in India, without exception."[84] Therefore, any wood exported from India under HS 4407 violates Indian law. The affidavit also indicates that exporting wood veneers from India under HS 4408 is legal.[85]

What the Affidavit for the Gibson Warrants States

In order to obtain the search warrants, a Special Agent of FWS completed an affidavit outlining the basis for the search. Four search warrants were ultimately obtained to search Gibson's manufacturing, rough mill, and corporate locations, as well as to search a delivery service. Two shipments formed the basis for the Affidavit: a shipment of ebony from India on June 27, 2011;

(...continued)

decisions." See FSC website, http://www.fsc.org/about-fsc.html.

[82] *Gibson Guitar Corp. Responds to Federal Raid* (August 25, 2011), available at http://www.gibson.com/en-us/Lifestyle/News/gibson-0825-2011.

[83] Tariff classification ruling NY 881630 (January 26, 1993) (pertaining to sawn Indian rosewood (*Dalbergia latifolia*) and sawn Indian ebony (*Diospyros ebenum*)).

[84] John M. Rayfield, FWS, *Affidavit in Support of Search Warrant # 11-MJ-1067 A, B, C, D*, p. 4 (August 18, 2011) (hereinafter Affidavit). See also Affidavit, p. 8 ("Further research of ... all other published laws and regulations of the Government of India ... revealed no exceptions to this export prohibition").

[85] Affidavit at 7.

---

and a shipment of rosewood and ebony from India on June 20, 2011, which was investigated after the June 27 shipment.[86]

June 27, 2011, Shipment

According to the Affidavit, a CPB official at the Dallas airport suspected a June 27, 2011, shipment of Indian ebony violated the Lacey Act and referred the shipment to an FWS inspector.[87] The FWS inspector, CBP officer, and the APHIS specialist physically identified the shipment as containing sawn Indian ebony of a thickness of 10 mm described under HS 4407.[88] Multiple pieces of documentation accompanied this shipment. (See **Table 1**.) The information on the documents was not consistent, identifying different HS codes (for veneer, for fingerboards, for completed musical instrument parts); and different importers (one in Germany, one in Canada, and Gibson).

Table 1. Documentation Accompanying June 27, 2011, Shipment

Document	Contents as Declared on Form	HS Number	Ultimate Receiver of Goods	Other Information
Air Way Bill 589 2025 5804			Theodor Nagel, Gmbh (of Germany)	Contact Luthier Mercantile upon import. Marked for direct transport to Nashville, TN
Customs and Border Protection Form 3461 (U.S. Customs entry declaration)	Veneer Sheets less than 6 mm	HS 4408.90.0195	Luthier Mercantile (of Canada)	
Indian export declaration (June 10, 2011)	Indian ebony	HS 9209.92.00 (finished parts of musical instruments)		
Certificate of Origin from India	Indian ebony finger boards, 10 mm thick		Nashville Airport	
Lacey Act Declaration (USDA Form PPQ) (June 17, 2011)	Ebony fingerboards for guitars: *Diospyros ebenum*, harvested in India.	HS 4407.99.96	Gibson Guitar Corp.	Document submitted after shipment was referred to FWS for investigation on June 27, 2011

Source: Congressional Research Service, based on information from John M. Rayfield, FWS, *Affidavit in Support of Search Warrant # 11-MJ-1067 A, B, C, D*, pp. 9-11 (August 18, 2011).

Note: Blanks in the Table indicate that information was not available, but do not suggest that information was required.

---

[86] Neither Indian rosewood (*Dalbergia latifolia*) nor ebony (*Diospyros ebenum*) appear to be species protected under the Convention on International Trade of Endangered Species of Wild Fauna and Flora (CITES) or other American law.

[87] Affidavit at 8.

[88] Affidavit at 8, 11.

The only form that identified the contents as being under HS 4407 and the ultimate receiver being Gibson, according to the information in the Affidavit, was the Lacey Act declaration submitted by Gibson. The declaration was submitted after the investigation had started. That declaration indicated that the shipment for Gibson contained ebony fingerboards under HS 4407. The problem is that India prohibits export of wood under HS 4407, according to the Affidavit. If the Gibson declaration is true, India export law has been violated. If India export law has been violated, it is possible that the predicate violation of the Lacey Act has been triggered and that a violation of Section 3372(a)(2)(B)(iii) has occurred. As discussed above, that section states that a Lacey Act violation has occurred if an item has been imported, exported, transported, sold, received, acquired, or purchased in interstate or foreign commerce and that item was taken, possessed, transported, or sold in violation of a state or foreign law that governs the export or transshipment of plants. There are no statements in the Affidavit regarding an Indian law protecting ebony or requiring royalties or fees, and thus it appears that FWS is not making a case that there is a violation of either Section 3372(a)(2)(B)(i)—pertaining to foreign laws protecting plants; or Section 3372(a)(2)(B)(ii)—pertaining to foreign laws requiring payment of royalties, taxes, or stumpage fees. Any certification by the Forest Stewardship Council of the timber product would seem irrelevant, as forestry practices do not appear to be the issue in this case.

June 20, 2011, Shipment

The Affidavit also recounts facts relating to an earlier shipment that was discovered after the June 27, 2011, shipment. Again, CPB alerted FWS to a possible Lacey Act violation, in this case Indian rosewood and Indian ebony imported on June 20, 2011.[89] The details about this shipment's documentation are not as clear as for the June 27 shipment. However, the Affidavit indicates that the U.S. customs import declaration identifies Luthier Mercantile as the ultimate receiver of the goods, but that an email from Luthier Mercantile identified Gibson Guitar as the importer.[90] The Affidavit indicates that the shipment was "sawn Indian ebony and sawn Indian rosewood imported under HS code 4407."[91]

While Indian rosewood does not appear to be a protected species under CITES or the ESA, other types of rosewood do have import limitations. CITES lists Brazilian rosewood (*Dalbergia nigra*), Honduran rosewood (*Dalbergia stevensonii*), and Nicaraguan rosewood (*Dalbergia retusa*), thus restricting their trade. No similar restrictions of ebony were found.

Other Shipments to Gibson

The Affidavit indicates that prior to these two shipments, Gibson has submitted Lacey Act declarations for wood products from India eleven times since August 2010.[92] According to the Affidavit, the CPB database shows eleven shipments of rosewood and/or ebony from India to Gibson under HS 4407.[93] FWS brought a forfeiture action related to a Gibson import of ebony from Madagascar in 2009.[94]

---

[89] Affidavit at 14 (stating the shipment was discovered on July 28, 2011).

[90] Affidavit at 14.

[91] Affidavit at 14.

[92] Affidavit at 11-12.

[93] Affidavit at 12-13.

[94] United States v. Ebony Wood in Various Forms, No. 3:10-cv-747 (M.D. Tenn. *administratively closed* September (continued...)

If Gibson is charged under Section 3372(a)(B)(iii) for any of these shipments, rather than DOJ proceeding with a civil forfeiture action only,[95] DOJ would need to show that Gibson *knew* that the shipment violated a law related to export. It would not have to show that Gibson knew the specific Indian law, only that it was doing something illegal.[96] According to the Ninth Circuit, the Lacey Act does not require "that the violator know all the details of the statutes and regulations that make the conduct unlawful. It suffices that he knows, not only that he is importing or exporting [the plant or animal], but also that the [plants or animals] are tainted by a violation of some law."[97] A court may consider Gibson's business importing wood;[98] that it has been charged with an import violation before;[99] and/or that the documentation was inconsistent (perhaps to conceal the violation) as evidence that Gibson knew the import was against the law.

Legislation in the 112th Congress

The 112th Congress is considering legislation to alter the Lacey Act. On October 17, 2011, an amendment was proposed to an agriculture appropriations bill that targeted agency funding:

> None of the funds appropriated or otherwise made available by this title shall be used to pay the salaries and expenses of personnel to enforce the provisions of section 3(a)(2) of the Lacey Act Amendments of 1981 ... with respect to a plant taken, possessed, transported, or sold in violation of a foreign law unless the applicable foreign government has initiated proceedings against the company or individual under the foreign law.[100]

This would have affected APHIS enforcement had it passed, but would not have restricted FWS or CBP funding, neither of which are under the Department of Agriculture. By requiring foreign enforcement before U.S. enforcement were possible, this amendment would have reversed over a century of Lacey Act precedent.

Two other bills regarding the Lacey Act are pending. H.R. 3210 would limit the application of the 2008 Amendments. It would amend the act to provide statutory protection for plant or plant products assembled or imported prior to the date the 2008 Amendments were enacted.[101] This would serve as what is commonly called a *grandfather clause* for actions prior to May 22, 2008. While the 2008 Amendments did not take effect before that date, the law does not have an

---

(...continued)

28, 2011). See Heath E. Combs, *Gibson Raid Raises Attention on Lacey Act Enforcement*, Furniture Today (September 6, 2011), available at http://www.furnituretoday.com/article/print/542690-Gibson_raid_raises_attention_on_Lacey_Act_enforcement.php.

[95] Forfeiture action has been filed. United States v. 25 Bundles of Indian Ebony Wood, No. 3:11-cv-913 (M.D. Tenn. 2011).

[96] See, e.g., United States v. Santillan, 243 F.3d 1125 (9th Cir. 2001) (holding that culpability was demonstrated by the fact that he lied about the parrots he was hiding in his car while crossing into the United States from Mexico).

[97] United States v. Santillan, 243 F.3d 1125, 1129 (9th Cir. 2001).

[98] See United States v. Three Pallets of Tropical Hardwood (Crouch), INV. No. 2009403072, at 5 (Office of the DOI Solicitor June 22, 2010) (rejecting a defense that the declaration requirement was new, holding that "a company that specializes in international shipments should be well versed in the applicable laws that govern such transactions").

[99] See United States v. Kuipers, 49 F.3d 1254 (7th Cir. 1995) (allowing DOJ to introduce other crimes in a Lacey Act case to show defendant *knew* he was violating the law).

[100] S.Amdt. 765 to H.R. 2112 (112th Congress).

[101] H.R. 3210, §3.

---

effective date for when the predicate action may have occurred. Accordingly, without the provision proposed in H.R. 3210, Section 3, if a musical instrument was sold in 2010 made of wood that was illegally taken in 2002, that sale violates the Lacey Act. APHIS has proposed regulations that would revise the declaration requirement for pre-2008 material.[102] Additionally, as discussed above, the Lacey Act requires knowledge of or reasonable care to discover the underlying violation, so only those buyers and sellers who knew or should have known of the underlying problem would be subject to prosecution. Additionally, the Director of FWS has stated that the agency is not pursuing enforcement against owners of instruments, but is focusing on importers.[103]

Section 3 of the bill would also assist innocent owners by excluding the CAFRA provision that blocks the innocent owner defense for contraband or goods taken illegally. Innocent owners could also be aided by Section 7, which would authorize a certification program so that plants and plant products could be certified as legal for the purposes of sale and resale.

H.R. 3210 also would limit the types of wood that were covered by the declaration requirement. Section 3 would require a declaration only for wood that was "entered for consumption." The designation of "entered for consumption"[104] applies to wood products that will be used in commerce once they enter the United States and are not for personal use only. This appears intended to exclude people transporting musical instruments for personal use from the declaration requirements. Section 3 also would change the declaration condition for providing scientific name, the value and quantity, and the country of origin, requiring only solid wood importers to complete that information. Particle board and medium density fiberboard importers would no longer have to detail where their composite wood came from. To the extent that composite wood is made of spruce, pine, or fir, APHIS has already proposed regulations to limit the declaration requirements.[105]

Section 4 of the bill would cap the civil penalty for a first violation at $250.

Section 5 of the bill would postpone the deadline of the APHIS report on the declaration implementation to 180 days after H.R. 3210 is enacted. The extended deadline would allow consideration of the changes from H.R. 3210. Section 5 would also direct FWS to evaluate the feasibility of providing a database of "laws of foreign countries from which plants are exported." No additional funding for these programs is provided by the bill.

H.R. 3210, Section 8 directs the Federal Trade Commission (FTC) to study the competitiveness of the U.S. market for raw materials that are used for musical instrument manufacture. The FTC report would be due 180 days after enactment.

Bills H.R. 4171 and S. 2062 take a different approach to amending the act. They propose excising all references to violations of foreign law from the Lacey Act, making actions illegal only if they have run afoul of state, federal, or tribal law. Accordingly, H.R. 4171/S. 2062 would effectively halt any protections the Lacey Act provided to the domestic timber industry from illegal foreign harvesting. The bills would also eliminate any criminal prosecutions, including the power to issue

---

[102] 76 Fed. Reg. 38330 (June 11, 2011).

[103] Daniel Ashe, Director, FWS, at a congressional briefing (September 28, 2011).

[104] 19 C.F.R. §141.0a.

[105] 76 Fed. Reg. 38330 (June 11, 2011).

warrants and make arrests, while capping civil penalties at $200,000, an amount smaller than the current criminal maximum penalty of $250,000 for individuals and $500,000 for organizations. They would alter the forfeiture proceedings by eliminating the incorporation by reference of customs laws. This would end the practice of administrative remission and allow only judicial claims for those seeking return of forfeited goods. The bills do not address the issue of strict liability for forfeitures.

Appendix. Declarations Enforcement Chart

Figure A-1. Phase-In Schedule of Enforcement of the Declaration Requirement for Goods of, or Containing, Plants or Plant Products

I December 15, 2008	II April 1, 2009	III October 1, 2009	IV April 1, 2010
PPS Plant Import Declaration Form will be available on Web site, and accepted after December 15, 2008. Domestic and International Outreach.	HTS Chapters: Ch. 44 Headings (wood & articles of wood) 4401—(Fuel wood) 4403—(Wood in the rough) 4404—(Hoopwood; poles, piles, stakes) 4406—(Railway or tramway sleepers) 4407—(Wood sawn or chipped lengthwise) 4409—(Wood continuously shaped) 4417—(Tools, tool handles, broom handles) 4418—(Builders' joinery and carpentry of wood)	HTS Chapters: Ch. 44 Headings (wood & articles of wood) 4402—Wood charcoal 4412—Plywood, veneered panels, except 44129906 and 44129957 4414—Wooden frames 4419—Tableware & kitchenware of wood 4420—Wood marquetry, caskets, statuettes	HTS Chapters: Ch. 44 Headings (wood & articles of wood) 4421—Other articles of wood Ch. 66 Headings (umbrellas, walking sticks, riding crops) 6602—Walking sticks, whips, crops. Ch. 82 Headings (tools, implements) 8201—Hand tools Ch. 92 Headings (musical instruments) 9201—Pianos 9202—Other stringed instruments Ch. 93 Headings (arms and ammunition) 9302—Revolvers and pistols 93051020--Parts and accessories for revolvers and pistols Ch. 94 Headings (furniture, etc.) 940169—Seats with wood frames Ch. 95 Headings (toys, games & sporting equipment) 950420—Articles and accessories for billiards Ch. 97 Headings (works of art) 9703—Sculptures
		PLUS PHASE II	PLUS PHASES II & III

Source: Congressional Research Service based on data from charts published by APHIS in 74 Fed. Reg. 45415 (September 2, 2009) and 74 Fed. Reg. 5911 (February 3, 2009).

Note: According to APHIS in both of the *Federal Register* notices referenced above, "the failure to submit a declaration will not be prosecuted, and customs clearance will not be denied for lack of a declaration until after the phase-in date above."

Author Contact Information

Kristina Alexander
Legislative Attorney
kalexander@crs.loc.gov, 7-8597